ELEPHANT
HAVE RIGHT OF WAY

Life with the Wild Animals of Africa

◆

BETTY LESLIE-MELVILLE

A DOUBLEDAY BOOK FOR YOUNG READERS

ALSO BY BETTY LESLIE-MELVILLE

DAISY ROTHSCHILD:
The Giraffe That Lives with Me

WALTER WARTHOG:
The Warthog Who Moved In

A Doubleday Book for Young Readers
Published by
Delacorte Press
Bantam Doubleday Dell Publishing Group, Inc.
666 Fifth Avenue
New York, New York 10103
Doubleday and the portrayal of an anchor with a dolphin are trademarks of
Bantam Doubleday Dell Publishing Group, Inc.
Text copyright © 1992 by Betty Leslie-Melville
photos on front cover, pages 1, 9, 15, 19, 22, and 27 copyright © 1990 Franke Keating
photo on page 32 copyright © 1990 Elsa Conservation Trust
photo on page 35 copyright © 1990 George Steele
photo on page 38 copyright © 1990 Davina Dobie
photo on page 44 copyright © 1990 Marion Gordon
All other photos copyright © 1990 Betty Leslie-Melville

Library of Congress Cataloging in Publication Data

Leslie-Melville, Betty.
Elephant have right of way/by Betty Leslie-Melville;
photographs by Betty Leslie-Melville.
        p.   cm.
   Summary: The author describes her experiences living in East Africa and
working to save the endangered species there.
   ISBN 0-385-30622-9
   1. Africa, East—Description and travel —1963–1992— Juvenile
literature.   2. Africa, East—Description and travel—1963–1992—
Views—Juvenile literature. [1. Zoology—Africa, East.
2. Wildlife conservation—Africa, East.   3. Africa, East—
Description and travel.]   I. Title.
DT426.L37   1992
967.6204—dc20   91-31258   CIP   AC

Design by Lynn Braswell

Manufactured in the United States of America
June 1992
10 9 8 7 6 5 4 3 2 1
WOR

To my delight—my grandson Rex,
who lives in Africa and helps me take care of Walter II.

Introduction

OPPOSITE:
*Betty Leslie-Melville, Daisy,
Marlon, and herd dog
Shirley*

I love Africa. I love living in Africa. One reason is that it makes me laugh. When I am way out in the bush among the animals, the game park traffic signs along the dirt roads say ELEPHANT HAVE RIGHT OF WAY. Since I don't see many signs like that in America, I think it is funny. But it means what it says because the African elephant can be very dangerous. So we always stop our car and wait, sometimes for a long time, for the elephants to cross the road.

Another reason I love living in Africa is that when I'm at home and wake up in the morning, a giraffe has its head in my second-floor bedroom window and she's looking at me with big brown eyes with long long eyelashes. Sleepily I call, "Good morning, Daisy," from my bed, then I walk over to her and give her a kiss on her forehead and rub behind her ears where her skin is as soft as velvet. When I go downstairs, a huge wild warthog has his head inside the front door. So I say, "Good morning, Walter," and give him a kiss and scratch his face which feels like sandpaper.

By this time Daisy has appeared at the front door too, wanting food, so I get some grain from a container we keep by the door and hold a handful out to each of them. They gobble it up gently and want more. So I get two more handfuls, and as I am feeding them, I see that standing on the lawn are five more giraffes and four baby warthogs and a zebra, and that soon I will be feeding all of them.

And those are just some reasons why I love living in Africa.

Afrika Mashariki,
the Most Beautiful Place on Earth

The front lawn at Giraffe Manor

But how did I get all the way to Africa to live, when I was born and lived in Baltimore? How did I come to have such an unusual life when I once lived like most other Americans? Well, I'll tell you.

I had a job teaching nursery school when something happened that changed everything. My best friend, who also taught at my school, decided to become a nun, so she joined an order in Africa.

Africa had always fascinated me. I had always wanted to go there, so I saved up my money and went to visit my friend in Tanzania, a country in Afrika Mashariki, which is Swahili for East Africa. It was the first time I had ever been on an airplane and I was scared, but when I finally got there after two whole days of flying I was very happy to see her.

During my visit I stayed in a hut with a tin roof out in a remote part of the country that in Africa is called the bush. Every night I heard the lions roar. There was no electricity. The legs of the wooden dining table stood in empty tin cans to keep the termites from eating the entire table. We ate hippoburgers, and they were very good.

My nun friend had opened a small school for African

Maasai schoolchildren and teacher

children. In order to be able to attend the children had to be five years old. Masses of children arrived at the school wanting to go, but because births are not recorded way out in the bush, they didn't know how old they were. So my nun friend would line them up and tell them to put one arm over their head and touch their ear on the other side. If they could reach their ear they could come to school; if not, they had to wait until they could. No child can reach his ear that way until he is five years old.

My friend also took the Africans medicine when they were sick. She brought me with her into their huts. The women in that tribe shaved their heads, so they had never seen long hair like mine before. They kept touching it and giggling. I loved all the Africans I met, they were all so nice and gentle. I loved everything about the country too. It was magnificent.

I fell in love with Africa.

When I got back to the United States, I told my husband I knew he would love it, too, so with our three children we got on a ship and sailed back to Africa. This time it took thirty-three days to get there.

Zebras out in the bush

We finally arrived in Kenya, another country in East Africa that borders on the Indian Ocean. As the ship docked, my six-year-old daughter looked around at all the beauty and asked, "Does God live here?"

We traveled all around the country in an open safari car and saw lions, elephants, rhinos, cheetahs, giraffes, and zebras. My husband and children fell in love with Africa, too, so we decided to move there.

So that's how I got to live in Africa.

Africa is vast. You can put the entire United States into Africa three and a half times. There are many countries, but we liked Kenya best. Living there is not too different from living in the United States. We lived in the suburbs of Nairobi, the biggest city in Kenya. Our house was made of white stucco and had a living room, dining room, a modern kitchen, three bedrooms, and a bath. The children went to schools a lot like the ones in America, and my husband drove into town to work every day. Sometimes we all went to town, saw a movie, ate at Kentucky Fried Chicken, and then went to Dairy Queen for dessert. We had a cat and a dog. The only difference was we also had big black monkeys with white faces that swung all over the trees in our yard and ate all the roses.

But again something happened that changed our lives. My husband and I went into the safari business and spent a lot of time driving Americans around in the bush on photographic safaris. During the day we showed them all the animals. At night we slept in tents.

Being around the animals so much, we came to love and respect them all. We also learned that some of them were becoming endangered.

Endangered species are animals that are threatened with extinction. Elephants and rhinos, for example, have lived in Kenya for millions of years. There used to be a lot of them, but now there are few because people kill them, so they have become endangered species.

Poachers are the people who kill the animals.

Elephants are killed for their ivory tusks. The poacher kills the elephant, then hacks out the ivory tusks from its head and sells them to people in other countries in the world who carve the ivory into bracelets and earrings and little trinkets. If people wouldn't buy things carved from ivory, the elephants wouldn't be killed.

Rhinos are killed for their horns, which are made into dagger handles by some Arabs. The rhinos wouldn't be killed if no one bought their horns. Cheetah and leopard skins are made into fur coats. Zebra skins are made into rugs. If people didn't buy things made from wild animal skins, the animals would not be killed.

If we don't stop this slaughter soon there will be no elephants, rhinos, zebras, leopards, or cheetahs left. They will have become extinct. After learning of this we wanted to help save the animals, but we didn't know how to go about it. Then yet again something happened that made this dream come true.

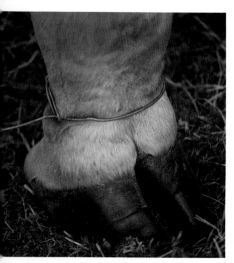

A giraffe's foot caught in a poacher's snare

Twiga,
the Tallest Animal on Earth

We moved to another house not too far away. Much to our surprise, the first evening we moved in, three big giraffes wandered down our driveway, nibbled at our trees, stayed for a while, then sauntered off. They came every evening. We grew very fond of them and named them Tom, Dick, and Harry. Although we could never get near them because they were afraid of us, we loved watching them.

A Rothschild giraffe

In Kenya there are three species of *twiga*, which is the Swahili word for giraffe. Tom, Dick, and Harry were Maasai giraffes. Their patterns are just sort of fuzzy spots. Another species is called the reticulated giraffe—their patterns are so precise, they look like a jigsaw puzzle put together. The third species is the Rothschild giraffe, which have sort of spotted patterns. Unlike the other two species, the Rothschild giraffes' spots don't go all the way down their legs. They are the only species with pure white legs from the knees down. They are also the largest species.

Giraffes are the only animals born with horns, and they all have three. (The bump in the middle of their forehead is actually a horn too.) The Rothschild males grow two more horns on the back of their heads. They used to be

OPPOSITE:
Daisy and a friend.
Can you find him?

called the five-horned giraffe until a man named Walter Rothschild registered them in his name.

The Rothschild giraffe became an endangered species because they were being poached. Africans were moving onto the same land with the giraffes and planting crops, and the giraffes were knocking their fences down and destroying their food.

We understood why the Africans were killing the giraffes but did not know what to do. Soon there were only 130 Rothschild giraffes left in the entire world.

Then one day a friend who owned the land up-country, where the last Rothschild giraffes lived, telephoned and asked us if we would take one of them, so there would be at least one of that species left. He knew, because of Tom, Dick, and Harry, that our land had the right kind of trees to feed giraffes.

We thought about this carefully. Wild animals are very difficult to raise. No one had ever been successful in raising wild giraffes before, but we knew if we didn't try they would all be gone. So we brought an adorable three-month-old baby giraffe to our property. I was slightly afraid of her at first. After all, giraffes are six feet tall when they are born and grow one eighth of an inch a day for the first year. They end up being eighteen feet tall—twice as tall as your ceiling. But I loved her anyway.

We built the little giraffe a nice enclosure, called a *boma,* and filled it with lots of hay to keep her warm and comfortable. We named her Daisy. Every day we gave her four huge bottles of milk and piles of leaves to eat. Most important of all we gave her lots of love. All day long we let her suck our thumbs, stroked her, and talked baby talk to her.

To stay alive animals must "imprint" on one creature. *Imprint* means "to bond with," to have someone they feel

they belong to who will love them and take care of them. Usually it is the animal's mother who takes care of it and gives it all that love, but if there is no mother, someone else must take her place.

For Daisy that creature was my husband. She thought I was okay, to her I was a herd member. But Daisy really loved my husband best.

When he'd go to work in the morning, she would just stand in one place on the lawn as if she were growing there, and wouldn't move until she saw his car come into the driveway. Then she'd run up to the car, put her head in the window, and give him a kiss. I felt sorry for her being alone all day, so I said we had to get another one to keep her company. And so we did.

This time we got a three-week-old male and named him Marlon. This little giraffe liked my husband, but he imprinted on me. He liked me best! He was also crazy about Daisy, but she was jealous and didn't like him at all at first. But eventually she became his friend too.

My husband and children and I have all grown to love Daisy and Marlon very much. They love us too. They come when called and go for walks with us. They look in the second-floor bedroom windows every morning to see if we are awake, and put their heads in the front door and over the dining-room table while we're eating. They take carrots from my mouth, which causes many visitors to ask with some disgust, "Oh, isn't that unsanitary?"

And I always answer them, "Yes, there's no telling what the giraffe might catch. They eat only leaves and have the cleanest mouths in the world."

As we learned how gentle and intelligent giraffes are, we really worried about all the rest of the endangered giraffes left on our friend's ranch and wanted to save each and every one of them. But we couldn't have all of them on our

*African schoolchildren
feeding Marlon*
FRANKE KEATING

own property because we didn't have enough trees for them to eat.

It costs a lot of money to save giraffes. First the game department has to tranquilize them, then take them to a large area that has to be fenced in. They must be left there for six weeks so they'll form a herd. Each giraffe also has to have a crate in which tree branches for them to eat are tied every day so they will go in the crates and get used to them. Then one day when they are inside eating, the door will be closed and the huge crates with the giraffes in them

loaded on trucks and moved to the safety of a game park.

The giraffes are then unloaded into another fenced-in area where they must stay for six more weeks so they'll get familiar with their new surroundings, and then they are released—set free. The game department, the vets, the enclosures, the crates, and the trucks all cost a lot of money.

To raise the funds we formed a wildlife organization called the African Fund for Endangered Wildlife (AFEW), and wrote letters to people asking them to help. We gave "Save the Giraffe" parties in Kenya and all over North America. We raised enough money to move the first twenty-three to a game park where there were no other giraffes.

The giraffes liked their ride to the park. Their heads stuck up outside the crates and they looked all around, with great interest, at things they had never seen before. As we drove through a city, many African children squealed with delight when they saw them and ran after the trucks, waving to the giraffes all the way to the park. The giraffes loved their new home; they were safe there. Now they have bred and there are ninety-three of them.

We have also raised enough money to move almost all the giraffes left on the ranch to the safety of other game parks. So now they're not an endangered species anymore.

It is a good feeling to know you have saved an endangered species. It not only costs a lot of money to save animals, it takes a lot of work. We have worked very hard so far for fourteen years, but most good things do take a lot of effort.

People who save animals are called "conservationists," and that's how we became conservationists.

OPPOSITE:
Rothschild giraffe being
translocated to the safety of
Lake Nakuru Park

Faru,
the Most Endangered Species in the World

There are seven species of rhinos in the world; only one of the species is not endangered—all the others are. The black rhino, the only species in East Africa, is very endangered. There were 22,000 in Kenya in 1977, today there are fewer than 400. There are many conservationists in Kenya trying to help rhinos.

Everyone calls me the "giraffe lady." I know a woman who is called the "rhino lady." The rhino lady's real name is Anna Mertz. She solved our problem of trying to save a very funny rhino. This is what happened: One day we had a call from the game department telling us that they had captured a rhino because the Maasai, who are an African tribe, had complained that this rhino had wandered onto their land and was chasing them. Rhinos are very fierce and the people were afraid. So the game department had tranquilized this rhino and taken him to their headquarters in the game park near us. They called him Faru, which is the Swahili word for rhino.

But they didn't have enough money to build a proper boma for him. The one they had made was way too small and had no shade. It didn't even have a wallow, and rhinos love to wallow in mudholes.

Black rhinoceroses, usually called rhinos for short
FRANKE KEATING

The game department said they also did not have enough money for food for him. They wanted to know could we help?

Rhinos are extremely dangerous. I have seen more than one vehicle with a big hole right through the door where a rhino has turned it over. They attack anything that seems to threaten them. They will even charge a freight train. But once captured, rhinos are the easiest of animals to tame. They will eat from your hand in twenty-four hours and become sweet. After thinking it over, we decided to see what we could do. We made a nice big enclosure for Faru with lots of shade and a wallow, and every day we took him food. He became very sweet. When he would see us coming with food he would make happy little sounds, like a tiny puppy. He loved to see us, not only because we brought him food and scratched him all over, but also because he was lonely.

So we decided to move him to a game park a hundred miles away that had eleven other rhinos—ten females and one male. The game department crated him and put the crate on a truck and we all drove to Amboseli Park. When we opened the door of his crate, Faru walked out and

looked all around. He was very pleased to be free again, and we were all so happy that he could now go back to living in the wild with the other rhinos. When he caught sight of the other rhinos in the distance, he ran gleefully toward them.

But guess what? The other male would not let him on his territory and chased him away every time he tried to approach. But we all decided they would soon become friends, and we went home.

Later we learned that Faru was still wandering around by himself because the older male fought him all the time. Poor Faru was too scared of him to try to approach the group anymore. He was all alone again.

One day as he was walking around sad and lonely, he noticed a tent with lots of people in it. They were tourists on safari who gathered in the bar tent every evening for drinks before dinner. Since Faru had grown so used to people feeding and scratching him, he decided the people in the bar tent would make fine company. So he happily strolled into the tent.

Everyone inside screamed and hollered and ran out the back door. Their drinks flew up in the air and crashed to the floor. The tourists didn't know he wasn't a wild rhino who was going to charge them or might even kill them. But Faru couldn't imagine what all the fuss was about. He visited the tent again the next night and the night after that. He was only trying to be friendly, but of course the hysteria happened every night. The manager of the tent camp was furious and told the game department they had to move the "bar rhino," as he called him, out of Amboseli Park immediately.

Once again Faru was crated and this time moved 150 miles north to a ranch where Anna Mertz had formed a rhino sanctuary and was taking care of rhinos that had

Even though Faru is young, he is very wrinkled

FRANKE KEATING

been orphaned or wounded by poachers.

Anna introduced Faru to the others very slowly, and soon they all became very good friends. We went to visit him and he just loves it there. Not only is he happy and safe, he has become the number-one rhino in the group!

Thank goodness for Anna Mertz, the rhino lady.

But not all conservation projects are so successful.

In order to make sure that every rhino in Kenya wouldn't be poached, we decided to move some of them to a ranch in Texas. The ranch owner was taking care of animals from American zoos so we thought the ranch would make a good home.

We were able to get five rhinos to send to Texas. They were to be sent by airplane. Their air fare cost over a hundred thousand dollars, but we worked hard and raised it.

The rhinos were put in wooden crates with iron bars surrounding each crate. But they hated the crates. At the airport they tore all the wood sides to shreds with their horns—it was a good thing the bars were on those crates!

Imagine traveling on an airplane with cargo like this
FRANKE KEATING

A crane lifted the rhinos onto the plane, and the head of the game department sat in the back of the plane in the baggage compartment with them. He had tranquilized them, but he was still afraid they might escape into the passenger compartment. Rhinos are so strong, they could easily crash through the side of a plane. He said it was the worst flight he had ever had. If I had been getting on that plane and learned there were going to be five black rhinos on it with me, I would have run right off.

However, the rhinos arrived in New York safely, and we had a cargo airline, called Flying Tigers, meet the plane from Africa to transfer them to Texas. (I wanted to paint FLYING RHINOS on the plane, but no one would let me.)

We met the rhinos in New York, then flew on to Texas ahead of them. We met them when they arrived at the airport there. Their damaged crates were loaded on trucks that drove them to the ranch. When their crates were opened they were so relieved to get out, stretch, and walk around their large, grassy enclosure. They thought America was wonderful. They were very happy and everyone was very happy with them.

But within three months all five rhinos were sick. Their teeth fell out and they grew extremely thin. No vet could find out what was wrong with them. Within a year they all died. It was very sad.

Finally, months after they had died, the scientists learned that the well water that had been dug for the rhinos did not have the right kind of minerals in it for rhinos.

Of course no one knew this ahead of time, but we learned from our mistake and didn't send any more rhinos to Texas.

So we didn't succeed with that project; but if you don't try things, you know you won't succeed. Everyone fails at something sometime or other, but the important thing is not to give up. We didn't give up, we just kept on trying to think of other ways of saving the endangered rhinos.

A group of scientists had a meeting at our house to discuss the idea of tranquilizing the rhinos, then cutting their horns off. A rhino is valuable only for its horn, and if it didn't have a horn no one would poach it. But we decided that that wouldn't work. Without their horns rhinos couldn't protect their babies from lions, then if the poachers didn't kill them, the lions would.

What all the conservationists finally decided was that, since Anna Mertz's land could not support any more rhinos, the only way to save them from becoming extinct was to move them to the safety of game parks. There they are kept in large areas surrounded by electric fences so they can't get out. Guards would also have to stay on duty twenty-four hours a day so poachers couldn't get in.

That is exactly what is being done.

And am I glad we didn't give up, because it's working! y few rhinos are being poached now.

Ndofu,
the Biggest Animal in Africa

Sam and a few friends

Another conservationist is a friend of ours called Daphne Sheldrick. She lives across the valley from us. One afternoon my husband and I decided to visit her. As we were clambering through thick bush, a fully grown rhino suddenly appeared before us! Was I scared!

My husband laughed. "Don't worry—that's Sam, that rhino of Daphne's. He's tame." I was relieved, but I was still nervous. However, Sam the rhino merely glanced at us and continued walking on ahead of us going back to Daphne's. My husband had known we were close to her house and that we might meet up with Sam in the woods, but not telling me was his idea of a joke. (I didn't think it was very funny.)

Daphne raises baby rhinos and elephants that have been wounded by poachers or orphaned because their parents have been poached.

Daphne's husband had been game warden of Tsavo Park, a big game park in Kenya. I used to think game parks were about the size of our parks in the United States, but in Kenya they are huge. Tsavo is the size of New Jersey.

One of Daphne's orphaned babies

Tsavo when animals were wounded or orphaned Daphne used to take them to her house and raise them.

An elephant named Eleanor, a buffalo, an ostrich, and a rhino all used to take a walk with Daphne down the dirt road in Tsavo every afternoon. It was an amazing sight. Every time we saw them strolling along together we were astonished. They all loved her as she did them. They followed her everywhere.

Ndofu is the Swahili word for elephants. There are two kinds of elephants in the world—the Indian and the African. The African elephant is much larger than the Indian one and has bigger ears. The Indian elephant can be ridden or used for work. Most of the elephants in the circus are Indian. The African elephant is much more dangerous than the Indian elephant. If it is threatened, it will charge.

One time, some people were in a small Volkswagen on safari way out in the bush of a game park when they saw an elephant standing in the narrow dirt road they were traveling on. The elephant was happily eating leaves from a tree. Obeying the ELEPHANT HAVE RIGHT OF WAY signs in

OPPOSITE:
When an elephant sticks its
ears out like this, it's
getting ready to charge.
You'd better run!
FRANKE KEATING

OPPOSITE:
An elephant family
FRANKE KEATING

the park, the people stopped their car, and waited and waited. The elephant was in no hurry to leave, but the people were. They were trying to get back to their lodge by dark, which is also a rule you must follow in the bush. But as dusk approached, the elephant was still standing in their way. Another car had driven up behind them and was also waiting.

Finally, the people in the first car grew impatient and blew their horn. The elephant turned, looked down at the little car, and walked over to it. It put its tusks into the open window and out the other side, picked the car with the people up in the air, and tossed it into the bushes. The people in the car behind snapped a photograph of the Volkswagen lifted twelve feet high in the air by the elephant. Then the elephant merely continued to eat. When it finally wandered off to more delicious trees, the people in the second car scrambled to the upside-down car in the bushes. The people in it were bruised and upset, of course, but miraculously they were not seriously hurt. From then on they all knew the ELEPHANT HAVE RIGHT OF WAY signs mean exactly what they say.

African elephants are highly intelligent. When road engineers survey steep hills where a road is going to be built, they always find the measuring they do for the road gradient is exactly the same as the track the elephant have made and used for hundreds of years. So elephants are excellent road engineers.

I am afraid of elephants but I really do love them. The most frightened I have ever been was the time my husband and I were driving just outside a game park on a very rough dirt road. Suddenly we heard a noise so loud, it sounded as if an earthquake were racing toward us. It got closer and closer, and finally we saw that it was an enormous herd of elephants. I don't know where they were

going, but they were in a hurry. They were running as fast as they could go right toward us. We stopped our car, and as they crossed the road they just ran around the car in front of us and in back of us so close, they were almost touching it. We sat there for what seemed like a half an hour. It was as if the whole world were full of nothing but elephants. Was I glad when they finally disappeared. We later learned it was a herd of one thousand!

We decided they had probably been shot at by a poacher and were running to the safety of a nearby game park. They know the boundaries of the parks. Hunters have told me they will track elephants in a blocked off area where it was legal to hunt, but the elephants know what to do. They run toward a nearby game park. Once they get there, they will just turn and stand and look at the hunter as if to say, "Ha! You can't get us here."

All hunting was made illegal in Kenya in 1977, but twenty-five thousand elephants have been poached in the last few years. One thousand were poached last year. Now the African rangers are catching many of the poachers,

Poachers go after elephants' beautiful white tusks

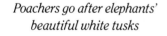

and they are thankful to the many people who send money to pay for their vehicles and their salaries. I am very glad to tell you that elephant poaching is now down.

Elephants are not only intelligent and majestic, they have fun too. One of the lodges in Tsavo Park consists of a series of small cabins with thatched roofs and little verandas. The elephants, out of curiosity, began wandering around the cabins. This scared the tourists. The manager decided to dig a deep moat around the area to keep the elephants away.

The first time the elephants appeared after the digging of the moat, they examined the fifteen-foot-deep pit for a few minutes, then sat down on their haunches and gleefully slid down into it. They looked so pleased, as if they were delighted a sliding board had been made just for them! Then they walked casually up the other side and scared tourists again.

After bumping into Sam the afternoon my husband and I were on our walk to Daphne's, we arrived there, greeted Daphne, then watched two little orphaned elephants romping around with their keeper.

Day or night, baby elephants never stop touching their mothers. The African keeper Daphne had hired for these two had become their mother. They had imprinted on him. He had to be there all day for them to touch, and he had to sleep with them all night too. I always assumed elephants had tough skin, but it is actually quite fragile. Baby elephants always stand under their mother's stomachs or under her enormous ears to protect their delicate skin from the sun. The mother elephant has an oily liquid in her nose that she sprays on the babies to keep them from getting sunburned. So the keeper at Daphne's had to put lots of coconut oil on these babies all day, and he smelled like coconut oil too.

The little elephants were so adorable, I wanted to touch them, but the day before a little boy who was visiting had put his finger into the mouth of one of the babies and the little elephant had bitten his finger off! The elephant hadn't meant to, he'd probably thought it was a carrot. But I decided I would just watch them nudging their keeper and playing with each other.

I wish I could have heard what the two little elephants were saying to each other, because elephants do talk to one another all day long. But it is a sound too low for humans to hear.

Eleanor, the elephant that used to go for a walk with Daphne at Tsavo, is the most extraordinary elephant in Kenya. She never had babies of her own, but when the young orphaned elephants Daphne raised at Tsavo were a little older and weaned from the bottles of milk she gave them, she would take them to Eleanor. Eleanor took care of the little things just as if they were her own.

After Daphne's husband died, she said a sad good-bye to Eleanor and her other animal friends, and moved to Nairobi where she became our neighbor. She now lives in a house in the Nairobi Game Park that the game department gave her. There she takes care of Sam and other wounded or orphaned animals. She always seems to have some baby elephants, rhinos, and antelopes.

When the orphaned elephants grow big enough to be weaned from their bottles of milk, Daphne takes them back to Tsavo Park and gives them to Eleanor. She still adopts them and takes care of them for about fifteen years, after which they go off on their own.

We have not only Daphne to thank for all the wonderful work she is doing to help save the animals, but Eleanor too—she's also a very good conservationist.

Simba,
the King of Beasts

I had a friend who lived in a cage.

His name was George Adamson. He lived among wild lions, and the cage kept them from attacking and killing him. It was just the opposite of a zoo—he lived in a cage and the lions wandered about free.

Simba is the Swahili word for lion. The female, the lioness, does all the hunting. She kills zebras, wildebeests, antelopes, and even buffaloes to eat. After she has made her kill, she roars to tell the male lion that dinner is ready. When he hears her dinner call, he races to the food and eats. He eats first—the female and the cubs just stand around and watch him. When he is finished the female eats, and then, and only if there is still some food left over, the cubs get to eat. If there isn't anything left for them, they starve and die. Sometimes their parents even eat them.

Many young lions die in the bush. However, in zoos around the world the zookeepers also feed the little lions along with the adults, so none of them die and there get to be too many lions for the zoos to keep.

George Adamson decided to take the surplus of young lions from the zoos that couldn't keep them and set them free in Africa. He moved to a remote place in Kenya where very few lions, but many camels, lived. There he raised some little zoo lion cubs and also lion cubs found starving in Kenya. He shot camels and fed the lions the camel meat.

When the lions grew up he wanted to set them free, but they didn't want to go. He would drive them way out in the bush, put them out of his Land-Rover, then leave them. But they would always walk back to his place. They didn't know how to kill, so they couldn't get any food.

I must tell you—lions are not very smart. Even if a leopard is *born* in captivity, to free it all you have to do is open the cage door. It will leap out and dash away and get its own food immediately—happy to be on its own. But lions raised by someone, even for a little while, don't know how to kill, and it takes a very long time to teach them. They are not only lazy, they don't learn quickly.

George Adamson taking a walk outside his cage
ELSA CONSERVATION TRUST

My son and I and the Hollywood lioness

But George would take them out to the bush day after day after day to teach them. When finally they did learn enough to get food for themselves, they would still come back to him—to get a free meal. Sometimes they would bring totally wild lions with them.

One of the wild ones mauled George, but he survived the attack and kept on raising lion cubs. He continued to live among the big ones he had raised, until recently when he died.

George is another person who did a lot of good work for conservation.

I would like to tell you a funny story about a lion. I have a photograph of myself and my son in front of our house in Nairobi with a fully grown lioness just lying at our feet! Everyone is astonished when they see it. But this is why I have it:

Some time ago my husband and I wrote a book about

our giraffes, which was made into a two-hour movie for television. It was filmed on our property. There was to be an episode in the film where a lion goes after a man on horseback who is trying to catch Daisy. Now, because lions in Africa are wild and dangerous, an animal trainer from California had to bring in a tame lion from Hollywood. This lion had been declawed and it always obeyed its trainer. We couldn't resist having our picture taken with the lion while it was at our house.

When the lion first arrived by plane from the States, a friend who lives in Kenya picked it up at the airport and drove it to our house in the backseat of his car. On the way he had to pass the Nairobi Game Park entrance, so he thought he'd play a joke on the game rangers. He stopped at the entrance gate and said to the ranger who came up to his car, "I was just driving from the airport and saw this lioness on the road, so I've brought her back to you."

Two wild lionesses

The warden looked into the backseat of the car, peered at the lioness just sitting there, and said, "It's not one of ours," and walked off.

There are about fifty-four lions in Nairobi Game Park and the wardens know what each and every one looks like and can tell them apart. Still, wouldn't you have thought he'd have been curious about where this lion came from? I mean, lions do not just roam the streets in the big city of Nairobi.

I must confess I do not like lions. I do not think they deserve to be called the "king of beasts." I think they are terrible parents and are also lazy and dumb. They're beautiful, but being beautiful on the outside is not enough. Being beautiful on the inside is what counts—and it turns you into looking pretty on the outside too.

Below you'll see a really beautiful animal.

Walter Warthog, my friend, who lives on our property. When people first see him they all exclaim, "Oh, isn't he ugly!" But he is so nice, smart, and affectionate, and takes such good care of his babies, that I now think he is truly beautiful. To know Walter is to love him, and to know how wonderful he is makes him beautiful to look at.
GEORGE STEELE

Duma,
the Fastest Animal in the World

I have another friend in Nairobi named Chryssee Martin, who had been asked by the game department to raise a sick and orphaned baby *duma,* the Swahili word for cheetah. Chryssee nursed the little cheetah back to health by giving it milk and something else cheetahs love to eat— guinea fowl eggs.

When it got better and grew a little, she went to the butcher every day and bought a fresh rabbit for it to eat. But, before she would give it to the cheetah, she would tie the dead rabbit to a stick and run with it. The little cheetah would run after the rabbit, grab it, and have a wonderful time playing with it. Chryssee did this every day so the cheetah would learn it had to chase and catch its own food. But the last time I saw it, it had no idea that chasing the rabbit was anything but a wonderful game.

When the cheetah does learn, Chryssee will release it to a safe place in the wild where it can be with other cheetahs and have babies.

Another friend in Nairobi named Davina Dobie was on safari when a game warden arrived at her tented camp with a baby cheetah whose mother had been poached. He had found the little thing just sitting in the middle of the

Chryssee Martin with her cheetah and VADM George Steele

bush under a tree all alone, looking very sad. He gave it to Davina and asked if she would take it to the game department in Nairobi.

Davina held the baby cheetah on her lap on the drive all the way back to Nairobi. By the time she reached the city she had fallen in love with it, and the baby cheetah had also become attached to her. Seeing this, the game department let her take the cheetah to her house to raise.

Cheetahs are the fastest animals on earth. They can run over seventy miles an hour. In fact, my favorite thing to see in the bush is a cheetah running. They look as if they are flying.

Davina named her little cheetah Chaos. It went with her everywhere—on a plane, in the car, to the drive-in movies, to dinner parties. Everyone loved it.

It grew and grew, and Davina loved Chaos very much. She knew cheetahs need lots of exercise, so she used to get on her horse and ride over open fields with Chaos running along beside her. But she knew Chaos needed more exercise than she was able to give it. She realized that the little cheetah should be able to run all day and that it needed to be free.

Another friend has an enormous ranch just outside of Nairobi, hundreds of acres all fenced in. There Chaos wouldn't be able to run onto the road. So, sadly Davina released her there. Davina cried all the way back to her house, but she knew Chaos would be much happier.

But within a few weeks Chaos had run into the fence, broken her neck, and died.

Sad things often happen with wild animals.

Chaos
DAVINA DOBIE

Punda Milia,
the Striped Donkey

We know a zebra isn't a donkey with stripes, but the Africans didn't have a word for zebra, so that is what they call them—*Punda Milia*, the Swahili words for "striped donkey."

There are two kinds of zebras in Kenya—Burchell's zebra and Grevy's zebra. There are many Burchell's zebras. These zebras are mean—they kick and bite. The Grevy are very gentle and nice. I have even ridden one. They look different from the Burchell's zebra too. Grevy's zebra have many more stripes—each has exactly one hundred. Their stripes are also much closer together than the Burchell's stripes. Their ears are much bigger and wonderfully fuzzy. Grevy's zebra is also an endangered species.

One day a Grevy's zebra limped onto our property. We were astounded to see this rare and endangered zebra because there isn't one within two hundred and fifty miles of Nairobi. Where had he come from?

We soon learned the answer—an animal trapper who had just moved down the valley from us had captured this one to sell to a zoo in Germany. The zebra had escaped and was hiding in our woods. He must have seen Daisy and Marlon and Walter Warthog in the woods and followed them onto our lawn.

When he saw my husband and children and me he was frightened, so he limped back into the woods. But he appeared again the next day and the next. He would just stand on the edge of the lawn and watch the giraffe and warthog with the saddest eyes I have ever seen. The giraffes had come from an area where no zebras lived, and they watched with great interest this odd animal who looked as if it were wearing pajamas. They all seemed to spend the day just staring at one another. Every evening the zebra would limp back into the woods. We assumed he must have hurt his leg escaping from the animal trapper.

Soon the zebra began to accept us, as long as we didn't try to approach him. I began putting a block of mineral salt, something all wild animals love to lick, on the ground every day when he arrived. Then I'd back up and sit on the ground myself so I would look smaller and less frightening to him. From what he considered a safe distance, he would look at the salt lick and then at me, but not come near it.

But every day he continued to watch the giraffes and the warthogs very closely as they came up to me and ate from my hand. After about a month he limped a few steps closer to me and the salt lick. He got close enough for me to see that he was a she, so I named her Zebrina. I talked to her softly all the time and kept telling her over and over again that we were her friends and loved her.

After a week or so of this she finally came up to the salt lick very slowly, all the time keeping an eye on me sitting not too far away. At last she licked it. This made us both very happy.

The next day I began putting grain on the ground for her too. She loved it and gobbled it up. Then I began holding it out to her in my hand. She would stretch her neck to reach the food, but at the last minute she'd lose her nerve and back off.

*Slowly Zebrina began to
approach us*

Then one evening, perhaps three months from the first time we'd seen her, Zebrina came up closer and closer to me, and this time put her head slowly down and gently took the grain from my hand! I was thrilled. And suddenly she didn't look sad anymore.

Zebrina moved in. She stayed with the giraffes all day and didn't go off into the woods at night anymore but slept right on the lawn next to Daisy and Marlon. She was so happy to have friends again.

Walter Warthog and Daisy and Marlon were all very nice to her—until the evening I put Zebrina's bowl of food next to Daisy's in Daisy's boma. When Zebrina walked in, Daisy was outraged. She walked over to Zebrina and kicked her with her front foot. Zebrina's eyes suddenly looked sad again.

I scolded Daisy and told her she had been very rude to Zebrina, but Daisy didn't care—she just kicked her again. Zebrina hobbled out sadly. I told Daisy that none of us really like to share, but since we want others to share with us, we have to pretend to like sharing even if we don't. But Daisy didn't pay any attention to me at all.

The next morning I put Zebrina's food back in Daisy's boma, and again Daisy kicked her. But this time instead of leaving, Zebrina turned around, put her rear end toward Daisy, and kicked Daisy with her back legs. Then she swiveled around to face Daisy as if to say, "What do you think of that?"

Daisy was startled. She thought a moment, then defiantly kicked Zebrina with her front legs once again, and Zebrina spun with great speed and lashed out with her back hooves again. Of course, neither of them was kicking with enough strength to do any harm. I just stood there laughing. They looked like two young girls having temper tantrums.

Finally Daisy gave up. Perhaps she just didn't want me to scold her again, but at least she let Zebrina eat in peace. Zebrina was delighted to be included.

Daisy and Marlon and Walter Warthog and my husband and children all became her herd. After all, we were the only other living creatures around and we were all very nice to her. She was so glad to have a herd again, even if we were all funny looking.

All these wild animals had moved onto our property and made friends with species, including humans, they had never known before. They were not captives or prisoners. There were no fences. They could have gone off anytime they wanted, but they all loved it there. They were loved, and fed good food, and most of all they felt safe. No one had tried to poach them. In fact, they thought no one would bother them at all there.

For many months no one did. Then one sad morning we awoke to find Zebrina was not on the lawn. She did not appear all day. We searched the woods to see if she was in a snare, but we couldn't find her or any trace of her anywhere. We were very upset.

The next day we had a call from Nairobi Game Park saying she was there. We drove over and found her—wounded. She had huge gashes on her nose where the poachers had captured her in a snare—which is a horrible wire trap. It had been a full moon the night she disappeared, which is when the poachers can see better to get their animal. But once again she had escaped somehow.

We tranquilized her, put her in a crate, and took her home. Was she happy to be back! We put purple medicine on her wounds and covered her up and left her in the stable with lots of comfortable hay where she would be warm and safe that night. But in the morning she was lying on the lawn with Daisy and Marlon. She had broken down the

*Dancy,
my daughter,
and Zebrina*

stable door to be with her friends.

Everything was back to normal in no time. We spent many happy days with her, the giraffes, Walter Warthog, and the children. But the next full moon Zebrina disappeared again, and we have never seen her since.

I am sure the poachers came back, and this time they got her.

Now she is somebody's rug.

We searched for her constantly for weeks, when I finally knew she wasn't coming back, I went down into the woods, sat on a log, and started to cry. Daisy came along. She leaned her head down over me, and as if she were sorry too, she licked the tears from my eyes.

The Game Department's capture unit tending to Zebrina's wound
MARION GORDON

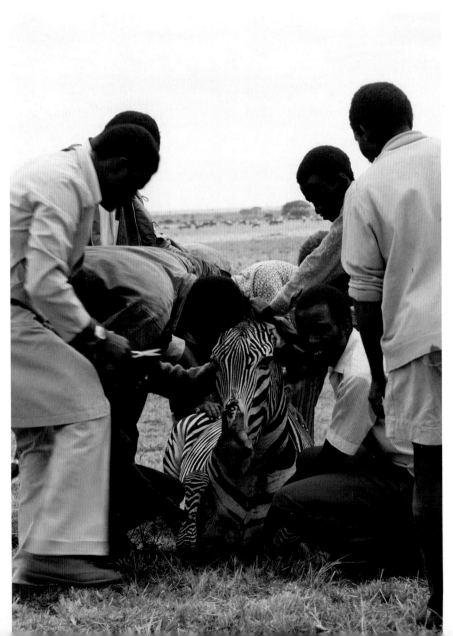

What Was an Elephant?

But despite the sad times I will keep on trying to save the animals. Saving just one wild animal is worth all the frustration. When you have saved an endangered species you know you have done something important and you really feel great. And although it costs a lot of money and time, you get paid in satisfaction.

People often ask me why we are saving animals when there are starving people in the world. That's a good question, but there is also a good answer. Saving the animals *is* saving the African people. I'll tell you why: Tourists come to Africa to go on safari in order to see the animals. This provides jobs for the Africans. Jobs not only for game rangers and wardens, antipoaching teams and vets, but also for drivers for the safari vehicles, guides for the tourists on safari, waiters in the safari lodges and tents, jobs for the people who build the roads to the lodges, jobs for the people growing the food for the tourists in the lodges. It is endless.

Most Africans are very poor and can't get jobs. But if they can get jobs and earn money, then they can buy food for their children. Then they won't have to poach the animals. If I were an African and my children didn't have anything to eat because I didn't have any money to buy them food, I would poach an animal for them to eat, too, wouldn't you? Even if they poach animals to sell the skins to others they usually eat the meat first. So even though it isn't right for the Africans to poach the game, it is understandable.

Many Africans didn't know they shouldn't poach the animals. So we decided to teach them. On our property we built the first education center in all of independent Africa. Every month now we bring over three thousand African schoolchildren to the education center, free, to let them

AFEW's Education Center

feed the giraffes and to teach them that without the animals, there will be no tourists, and without tourists they won't be able to get jobs.

The children love learning—they also love the giraffes. Many of them have never seen one before. Some of the very poor children who live in the city have never even seen a tree.

Many children who have read my books write to me and ask what they can do to help save the animals. There's a lot you children can do. You can tell everyone not to buy ivory—then the elephants won't be poached. You can tell everyone you know not to wear leopard skin coats or buy zebra skin rugs—then the leopards and zebras won't be poached. You can help educate the American people.

Since you don't live in Africa, you can't raise an orphaned elephant or rhino or giraffe, or be a game warden, or teach the Africans yourself. But you can raise money to help pay for the rangers to guard the rhinos, and pay the salaries of the antipoaching teams and the teachers who teach the children about conservation. For remember, the Africans are very poor and have no money for any of these things themselves.

Many African children whom we have taught, and many American children, are helping save the animals. They have thought of ways to raise money—they have made and sold cookies from door to door in their neighborhoods, they have put on shows and charged a dollar for each person to enter, they have sent fifty cents of their own allowance—for even fifty cents helps.

There is another reason to save animals. If all the giraffes and elephants and rhinos are killed, we humans can't make any more. And wouldn't it be awful if your grandchildren had to ask you, "What was a giraffe?," "What was an elephant?"

Index